For Helen R. Ross
D.R.
For Ee, Luke, and Hugh
J.N.

First edition for the United States and Canada
Published 1993 by Barron's Educational Series, Inc.

First published in 1993 by J.M. Dent, Orion House,
5 Upper St. Martin's Lane, London WC2H 9EA

All inquiries should be addressed to:
Barron's Educational Series, Inc.
250 Wireless Boulevard
Hauppauge, New York 11788

Library of Congress Catalog Card No. 93-12581

International Standard Book No. 0-8120-6350-3
International Standard Book No. 0-8120-9271-6
Library of Congress Cataloging-in-Publication Data

Ross, David, 1935–
     The serpent shell / David Ross ; illustrated by
Jan Nesbitt.
     p.   cm.
     Summary: While walking on the beach with his
grandfather, James asks to hear the story about
another young boy long ago who helped save a sea
serpent that was stranded on the beach.
     ISBN 0-8120-6350-3
     [1. Sea monsters—Fiction.   2. Seashore—
Fiction.   3. Grandfathers—Fiction.]   I. Nesbitt, Jan,
ill.   II. Title.
PZ7.R719643Se 1993
[E]—dc20   93-12581
                                                CIP
                                                AC

The illustrations for this book were prepared using
water-color and crayon.

PRINTED IN ITALY
3456   9985   987654321

THE SERPENT SHELL

David Ross
Illustrated by Jan Nesbitt

BARRON'S

"Come on, Grandpa," said James. "It's time for our walk along the beach. The tide has gone right out."

"Pull me up, then," said Grandpa. "Help me out of my chair. I'm not as young as I used to be."

When James stayed with his grandfather, they went walking on the beach every day, with Rory the collie. It was their favorite thing to do.

Outside, the sand stretched far away to the blue line of the sea.

"I can see the Mermaids," said James.

The Mermaids were three rocks that could only be seen when the tide was very far out.

"Tell me the story of the Sea Serpent and the Mermaids again," he said.

"Well now, once there was a boy, and his name was James too," Grandpa began. "He lived here by the sea all the time, not just on vacations like you. Sometimes at night he would lie awake, listening to the waves. He thought they sounded like the sea breathing. But one night he heard a voice calling: 'James-ey, James-ey,' very slowly. He thought it was the sea speaking to him."

"I'm called Jamesey, sometimes," said James, interrupting.

"So you are," said his grandfather.

"Shafts of bright moonlight came through the window as James got out of bed. The house seemed strange and quiet. Outside his room, the stairs were lost in a great well of darkness, but he knew his way down every step. The collie, asleep in his corner of the kitchen, opened one eye as James appeared, but did not stir. Noiselessly the boy tiptoed across to the door, opened it, then ran out, down to the end of the garden, through the little gate, and on to the beach.

"The tide was far, far out. James looked one way, and saw nothing but the empty beach. He looked the other way, and there he saw an enormous sea monster. It lay stretched out on the sand, great spiky fins rising from its backbone, its scales shining blue and green and silver in the moonlight, its crested head bent low. He heard the deep, slow voice again.

'Jamesey, will you help me?'

" 'How do you know my name?' asked James.

'I have watched you, in your father's boat, and I know you are a wise boy. I have heard him tell you about the creatures of the sea, the dolphins, the whales, and the great sea serpent.'

'Why do you need help?'

'I have been caught here by the mermaids,' said the sea serpent, its voice growing fainter. 'They are singing a song to keep the tide from coming in. If I cannot get back in the water, I will die, and they will take my scales for mirrors and my spines for combs. Can't you hear them, singing?'

"James listened. Yes, he could hear the mermaids. They sang in high voices, like a wind putting a spell on the waves, holding them back. He could see them, too, far off by the edge of the sea.

'What can I do?' he asked.

'Look on the sand,' said the serpent. 'If you can find a big seashell, perhaps I can still be saved.'

James hurried along the beach, searching. In the bright moonlight he saw starfish, jellyfish, small scuttling sand-crabs, but no shell. He had wandered very close to the mermaids now; they saw him, and beckoned, and called to him.

'Jamesey, come to us, to us!'

He could not help obeying, and went nearer still. But he heard the serpent moan, as it grew weaker, and suddenly he saw a shell like none he had seen before—big, spiky, and knobby. He picked it up and ran back as fast as he could, over the hard ripples of sand.

" 'Put the shell to your ear,' sighed the serpent. 'Can you hear the sea?'

'Yes,' said James. Inside the shell, he could hear the roar and crash of great waves breaking on coral reefs.

'At the pointed end of the shell is a little hole. Do you have plenty of puff in you, Jamesey?' The serpent's voice was only a whisper now.

'Then blow,' it said. 'Blow the sound of the waves back to the sea. Drown the seawitches' song, and the tide will come back.'

"But James could still hear the mermaids calling him. In his mind he saw their home at the bottom of the sea, a vast cave carpeted with green weed, gold and silver in its walls, shining with a pearly light. 'Welcome, Jamesey,' they said. 'Now you are ours.'

And they laughed, sitting on their thrones, surrounded by the bones of shipwrecked sailors. They combed their long hair with their spiny combs, and held up their shiny mirrors. And James fell under their power, and could not blow into the shell.

"Then he heard the sea serpent gasp beside him.

'Blow, Jamesey,'

He blew but no sound came out. The mermaids' song rose to a scream of rage as he shut his eyes and blew harder. A tiny sound came out, the merest sigh of an ocean breeze. James blew into the shell again, with all his strength. And the shell sounded out across the beach with a deep booming note.

"He kept blowing, with his eyes shut tight until he felt the cold water come lapping around his ankles. The song of the mermaids had stopped. The tide was coming in. James's cheeks were sore after all his blowing. He walked back up the beach, still clutching the shell.

Dawn was breaking over the horizon, and the moon was pale. The great sea serpent was swimming again, and its head rose from the water like a tower.

'You have saved my life, Jamesey. I will never forget it.' And as he watched, the serpent turned, and dived silently beneath the waves."

"Did he ever see the serpent again?" asked James.

"He never saw it again," said his grandfather. "But he was glad he had helped it. And the next time there was a very low tide, people saw three gray rocks they had not seen before. Because of their shape, they were called the Mermaids. But only Jamesey knew how they had come there."

"Didn't he tell anyone?" asked James.

"No, he kept it a secret for a very long time. Now, are you going to throw a stick for Rory to catch?"

When they were back in the little white house, James took the big shell down from the mantelpiece and held it to his ear.

"What can you hear in the shell, James?" James listened.

"I can hear big waves, far away," he said. "And I can hear a big voice, too. It says 'Jamesey, I have not forgotten.' "

James laid the shell down, very carefully, and looked at his grandfather, his eyes wide with astonishment.

"Jamesey was you, Grandpa, wasn't he?"

But his grandfather just smiled.

"It was all a very long time ago," he said.